ECT   B

FOR THE BENEFIT OF
HOCKEY FIGHTS CANCER

REFLECTIONS 2008

THE NHL HOCKEY YEAR IN PHOTOGRAPHS

presented by the **NATIONAL HOCKEY LEAGUE** and the

NATIONAL HOCKEY LEAGUE PLAYERS' ASSOCIATION

in conjunction with **NHL IMAGES** and **GETTY IMAGES**

GREYSTONE BOOKS

Douglas & McIntyre Publishing Group

Vancouver/Toronto/Berkeley

08 09 10 11 12   5 4 3 2 1

Greystone Books
A division of Douglas & McIntyre Ltd.
2323 Quebec Street, Suite 201
Vancouver, British Columbia
Canada V5T 4S7
www.greystonebooks.com

Library and Archives Canada Cataloguing in Publication
Reflections 2008 : the NHL hockey year in photographs/
presented by the National Hockey League and the National Hockey
League Players' Association in conjunction with Getty Images.
At head of title: For the benefit of Hockey fights cancer.

ISBN 978-1-55365-399-8

I. National Hockey League II. National Hockey League Players'
Association III. Getty Images, Inc

GV847.8.N3R44 2008   796.962´64   C2008-904898-9

Cover and interior design by Naomi MacDougall
Front cover photograph by Getty Images/Bill Wippert
Back cover photograph by Getty Images/Bruce Bennett
For a complete list of interior photo credits and captions, see page 159
Printed and bound in Canada by Friesens
Printed on paper that comes from sustainable forests managed
under the Forest Stewardship Council
Distributed in the U.S. by Publisher's Group West

We gratefully acknowledge the financial support of the Canada
Council for the Arts, the British Columbia Arts Council, the Province
of British Columbia through the Book Publishing Tax Credit, and
the Government of Canada through the Book Publishing Industry
Development Program (BPIDP) for our publishing activities.

DEDICATION

ALMOST EVERYONE KNOWS someone who has been touched by cancer—our hockey family is no exception. Many current and former members of the National Hockey League and their families have experienced the effects of the disease.

In December 1998, Hockey Fights Cancer was founded by the NHL and the National Hockey League Players' Association to raise money and awareness for the fight against cancer. This joint initiative is supported by NHL Member Clubs, NHL Alumni, the NHL Officials' Association, Professional Hockey Trainers and Equipment Managers, corporate marketing partners, broadcast partners, and by hockey fans throughout the world. To date, Hockey Fights Cancer has raised more than $10 million and a portion of the proceeds from this book will be donated to this important cause.

In October 2007, the NHL launched the "Hockey Fights Cancer—10th Anniversary" message board on its official blog site, NHL Connect. The forum was created for hockey fans around the world to share their experiences in the fight against cancer. More than 300 users joined the group. Below are just a few of the personal messages left on the board.

"My little sister, who is four years old, has leukemia. This is her second year off treatment, and we are loving it. She has considerable damage from the chemo but we make it work. I wanted to say thank you to the Columbus Blue Jackets who sponsor 'Hats for Heroes,' and the NHL in general. What you do makes the difference between a black day, and a spark of light."

AURORA AND AVALON H., OHIO

"My dad took me to my first hockey game. It was the Minnesota North Stars (yeah, it was a while ago) and taught me the love of hockey. I lost him March 19, 2003 to cancer. Every game I watch I can still hear him cheering…"

HEATHER D., FLORIDA

"It's great to see a sport go all out for people. With so much negativity in other sports, the NHL is a beacon of light. Hockey Fights Cancer is another reason why the NHL and all the players are top notch!"

MICHAEL H., VIRGINIA

"It is great that the greatest and toughest sport is lending its hand to fighting a tough disease."

SPUD, TENNESSEE

"We support any charity events that raise money for cancer research. Such a good cause and I think it's brilliant an organization such as the NHL is seen to be backing such a good cause."

PAUL B., UNITED KINGDOM

"I myself have just been diagnosed with cancer only a week or so ago, and you can imagine my shock and how scared I am right now, especially since I don't have any immediate family close by. I am so glad a big organization like the NHL is involved in research for this disease, because it hits almost everyone in America in some way or another. It was never a reality for me until the doctor said those words, and now I have to deal with it on the most personal of levels. So thank you, Hockey Fights Cancer— you have a new meaning in my life now."

JOCIE W., FLORIDA

"Real men wear pink. The fight against cancer is everybody's fight."

GERALD L., CALIFORNIA

Reflections 2008 is dedicated to those in the hockey community who have struggled, or continue to struggle, with cancer. We honour all the brave patients and their loved ones, and all of those who are searching for a cure.

REFLECTIONS—
A YEAR IN REVIEW

BY ROCKY BONANNO, NHL.COM

EVERY NHL SEASON has its constants: 1,230 games, 16 play-off teams, one Stanley Cup champion. What defines one season from another, what gives each its unique character, are those moments—the record setting goals, the stunning saves, the thrilling overtime victories—that pop before the eyes of hockey fans like flashbulbs.

The 2007–08 season was no exception—and the fans came out in droves to witness it all. For the first time in history, league-wide attendance surpassed 21 million, a per-game average of more than 17,000, marking the third consecutive season of growth.

And if you need proof of the commitment of NHL fans, look no further that last season's outdoor contest between the Buffalo Sabres and the Pittsburgh Penguins. What would possess 71,217 fans to sit outside for hours on a frigid day in upstate New York on January 1? For many, it was the opportunity to watch great hockey played in its purest form—in the great outdoors. A setting like this evokes memories of childhood and playing on a frozen pond for

hours upon hours until Mother came calling to announce dinner was on the table.

More than four years after the first outdoor game—the Heritage Classic, staged in Edmonton—the Sabres hosted the Penguins at Buffalo's Ralph Wilson Stadium, a football venue converted into a hockey arena for one very special day.

"Many of our players have great memories of playing outdoors when they were growing up," NHL Commissioner Gary Bettman said. "This game provides a wonderful opportunity to showcase our great players, honour hockey's heritage, and ring in the new year with the best fans in sports."

With snow falling throughout the game, the teams remained tied 1–1 following regulation and overtime. In the shootout, Pittsburgh's Sidney Crosby slipped the puck through goaltender Ryan Miller's pads for the game-deciding goal.

"Growing up, I played a lot outside," said Crosby, a native of Nova Scotia. "When you see 70,000 people jammed into a stadium to watch hockey, it's a good sign. The atmosphere and environment, I don't think you can beat that."

This past season, the league also put on a show for its international fanbase. The first ever regular-season NHL games were played in Europe as the defending Stanley Cup champion Anaheim Ducks met the Los Angeles Kings in a two-game series at the O2 Arena in London to launch the 2007–08 season.

"This was an opportunity to dip our toe in the water in Europe, take what we believe is the most international of the North American sports, and bring it to the other side of the Atlantic," Commissioner Bettman said.

THE NHL's 90th anniversary season opened its North American slate with a thrilling start as three of four games went to overtime. Less than a week later, though, hockey fans' thoughts turned from excitement to concern. On October 8, it was revealed that the Toronto Maple Leafs' Jason Blake was diagnosed with chronic myelogenous, a rare but treatable form of leukemia. The announcement was a sobering reminder of why the NHL established the Hockey Fights Cancer charitable program. The 34-year-old forward began treatment with medication immediately and, amazingly, didn't miss a single game, scoring 15 goals and 52 points in a trying season.

It was the second time cancer touched the Blake family. Jason missed the last 13 games of the 2000–01 season to be with his pregnant wife, who was diagnosed with thyroid cancer. She gave birth in April 2001, two weeks early, to a girl and later had throat surgery to remove a tumour that turned out to be benign.

At the NHL Awards Show in Toronto on June 12, Blake was awarded the Bill Masterton Memorial Trophy as the player who best exemplifies the qualities of perseverance, sportsmanship, and dedication to hockey. On the morning of the awards show, Blake visited his doctor and was told he would live a long healthy life.

"It's sad to say that you almost need something of this magnitude to make you realize how important each day is," Blake said.

BACK ON THE ICE, the season's opening month featured some special moments. The Kings' Brady Murray didn't have to get a ticket for his father to witness his NHL debut because Dad, Andy Murray, was in his usual position behind the bench as coach of the St. Louis Blues. This was the fourth instance in league history of a father coaching against his son. Dad's team earned a 5–3 road victory.

On October 7, Joe Sakic, the heart and soul of the Quebec/Colorado franchise, recorded his 1,591st career point to pass Phil Esposito for eighth place on the all-time scoring list. Sakic also passed Bobby Hull for sole possession of 14th place on the all-time goal-scoring list when he netted his 611th. Just under three weeks later, Sakic became the eighth player in NHL history to score 1,600 regular season career points. Injuries kept Sakic off the ice for 38 games soon after, but he returned in time to become the 11th player in NHL history to record 1,000 career assists.

Another goal-scoring record was set early in the season: For the first six games of the season, a Calgary Flames player produced a two-goal game, setting a modern-day NHL record previously held by the Buffalo Sabres (1992–93) and the Ottawa Senators (1917–18 and 1920–21). Daymond Langkow and Kristian Huselius reached the multi-goal mark twice each, and Matthew Lombardi and Jarome Iginla once each.

Meanwhile, Toronto captain Mats Sundin accomplished two astonishing feats with one whip of his stick on October 11. During an 8–1 home victory against the New York Islanders, Sundin became the all-time franchise leader in goals (390) and points (917), surpassing Darryl Sittler in both categories. Sundin was voted the first, second, and third star of the game.

IT WAS A PROUD YEAR FOR USA HOCKEY as two American-born players joined one of the NHL's most prestigious fraternities—the 500-goal club. On November 10, Boston native Jeremy Roenick scored the winning goal for San Jose in a 4–1 home victory against

Phoenix to become the 40th player to net 500. Roenick became the third American-born player to reach the mark, joining Mike Modano and Joe Mullen. By the end of 2007–08, fellow Massachusetts native Keith Tkachuk became the fourth American to join this club. His empty net shorthander late in the third period capped St. Louis' 4–1 win at Columbus on the final day of the regular season.

"You're just trying to survive and make it in the NHL," said Tkachuk, who debuted with the Winnipeg Jets in 1991–92. "Sixteen years later, you look back at a number, a lot of hard work by your parents, and the people around you ... and all the great players I played with, they're the reason why I'm in this situation."

Perhaps the greatest achievement by an American-bo rn player in 2007–08 occurred when Modano became the NHL's all-time leading American scorer. He scored twice in the first period of a 3–1 victory against the San Jose Sharks on November 7, giving him 1,233 points, one more than Phil Housley.

THE 500TH CAREER regular-season victory for Martin Brodeur was one of the more historically significant moments of 2007–08, as the mark had been reached only once before in league history. On November 17, the New Jersey goaltender joined Patrick Roy in the exclusive club by making 26 saves to defeat the Philadelphia Flyers

6–2 at Wachovia Center. Unlike Roy, Brodeur recorded every victory while playing for one team. He finished the season—his 15th—with 538 victories, only 13 behind Hall of Famer Roy (551).

If the Hockey Hall of Fame in Toronto needs to pick a captain for its next old-timers game, it'll have four more to choose from following the enshrinement of the 2007 induction class. On November 12, two of the highest-scoring centers—Ron Francis and Mark Messier—and two of the hardest-shooting defensemen—Al MacInnis and Scott Stevens—in NHL history increased the Hall's membership in the players category to 228. They combined for mind-boggling numbers of 1,779 goals, 5,867 points, and 12 Stanley Cup titles. Joining these four in the Class of 2007, as founder, was Jim Gregory, former Maple Leafs general manager and current senior president, hockey operations for the NHL.

Hall of Fame coach Al Arbour received an honour of a different kind in 2007–08. Two days after his 75th birthday, Arbour went behind the bench for the first time since June 2004 to coach his 1,500th game for the Islanders. The move was made possible when then-current coach Ted Nolan graciously offered to step aside for one night. On November 3, Arbour led the Islanders to a 3–2 victory against the Pittsburgh Penguins at Nassau Coliseum. Arbour previously guided New York from 1973–74 through 1985–86 and from December 1988 through 1993–94, winning four consecutive Stanley Cups in the early 1980s. A banner commemorating Arbour's 739 previous Islanders wins was lowered after the game, replaced by one with his name and the number "1,500."

Three players received the ultimate team honour in 2007–08 when Brian Leetch of the New York Rangers and Larry Robinson and Bob Gainey of the Montreal Canadiens had their numbers retired by their teams. Robinson, a Hall of Fame defenseman, won six Stanley Cups, two Norris Trophies, and a Conn Smythe Trophy with Montreal. His number 19 was the 12th in franchise history to be retired. Leetch, whose number 2 was the fifth retired in franchise history, holds team records with 741 career assists and ranks second in career points (981) and games played (1,129). He won the Stanley Cup, the Calder Trophy, two Norris Trophies, and the Conn Smythe Trophy in his Rangers career. Gainey's number 23 joined Robinson's 19 in the Bell Centre rafters. In his 16-year career with the Canadiens, which included eight seasons as captain, Gainey won five Stanley Cups, four Selke Trophies, and one Conn Smythe Trophy.

THE CEREMONIES for Robinson and Gainey reminded Montreal fans of the Canadiens' illustrious past. The nearly 100-year history of the Canadiens encompasses many memorable contests, but never before had they recorded an accomplishment like the one achieved on February 19, 2008. Trailing 5–0 in the second period against the New York Rangers, Montreal rallied with five consecutive goals before Saku Koivu's game-deciding shootout goal completed a wild 6−5 victory at Bell Centre. The Canadiens were down 5−0 after only 25 minutes, but netted two goals each from Michael Ryder and Alex Kovalev, and one from defenseman Mark Streit. Kovalev's second tally tied the score 5−5 at 15:38 of the third period. This tied the NHL record for the largest deficit overcome to win a regular season game, a feat last achieved by the St. Louis Blues in a 6−5 overtime victory against the Maple Leafs in Toronto in 2000.

In another game to remember, Minnesota Wild star Marian Gaborik treated fans at Xcel Energy Center on December 20 to a rare five-goal game, becoming the 42nd NHL player to accomplish the feat. The Wild defeated the Rangers 6−3. For good measure, Gaborik assisted on Pierre-Marc Bouchard's goal to finish with a six-point night, tying his career high. Gaborik's five-goal outburst was the first since Sergei Fedorov of Detroit burned Washington in 1996.

Ottawa captain Daniel Alfredsson was just as devastating to the Tampa Bay Lightning on January 24, scoring three goals and assisting on four others in an 8−4 rout at St. Pete Times Forum. He scored on the power play, shorthanded, and at even-strength. He also recorded the 500th assist of his 12-year career. Alfredsson's seven points were the most scored in one game in the NHL since Jaromir Jagr went 3-4-7 for Washington against Florida in 2003.

In spite of all these numeric milestones, 2007−08 may best be remembered for one number: 65. Alex Ovechkin, a third-year left winger, electrified crowds in every city the Washington Capitals visited. The Moscow native totalled 65 goals and 112 points, becoming the nineteenth player in NHL history to score at least 60 goals in a season. But instead of talking about his 65 goals—a total not reached in the league in over a decade—Ovechkin often sought to shift attention to the team's 43 victories, each one needed to give Washington its first postseason berth since 2002−03.

THE DRAMA AND EXCITEMENT of the regular season carried over to the 2007−08 Stanley Cup Playoffs. What better time for dramatic moments than in Game 7 of an NHL playoff game? The 2007−08 Quarterfinals produced three such games.

On April 21, Carey Price made 25 saves in Montreal's emphatic 5−0 defeat of Boston at Bell Centre. The Kostitsyn brothers—Andrei and Sergei—totalled three of the five tallies and each added an assist.

The following night, Washington hosted Philadelphia in Game 7 at Verizon Center in an overtime thriller that ended with Joffrey Lupul's power-play goal for a 3−2 Flyers victory. It was the 30th Game 7 decided in overtime in NHL playoff history. Who says home ice is an advantage? Philadelphia was the 15th road team to win one of these pivotal games.

In San Jose, Roenick scored twice and added two assists, and Evgeni Nabokov made 19 saves to lead the Sharks to a series-clinching 5–3 victory against the Calgary Flames at HP Pavilion. Roenick upped his career Game 7 goal total to six, which puts him in a tie for second most in NHL postseason history, only one behind Glenn Anderson.

Detroit's Johan Franzen was a sometimes-hot-sometimes-not goal scorer during the regular season. The Red Wings were delighted that one of his productive outbursts came when it was needed most—during the playoffs. He scored two goals in the first round against Nashville, nine against Colorado in the Western Semifinals, and two against Pittsburgh in the Stanley Cup Final, for a final tally of 13 goals in 16 games. Franzen's performance against the Avalanche was record setting. He established an NHL playoff record for most goals in a four-game series with nine. With hat tricks in Games 2 and 4, Franzen became the first player to record two or more hat tricks in one postseason series since Jari Kurri had three three-goal games for Edmonton against Chicago in 1985.

On May 4, the Dallas Stars hosted San Jose in Game 6 at American Airlines Arena, needing only one victory to eliminate the Sharks and advance to the Western Conference Finals. Easier said than done. Brenden Morrow, the Stars captain, scored a power-play goal at 9:03 of the fourth overtime to end the eighth-longest game in NHL history, giving the Stars a 2–1 series-clinching victory. Morrow deflected a pass from defenseman Stephane Robidas past Nabokov. It was the fourth overtime game in the series, three won by Dallas, two on goals by Morrow, and the fifth game decided by one goal. The contest lasted five hours and 17 minutes—long enough for Dallas goaltender Marty Turco to make a franchise-record 61 saves. Nabokov stopped 53 shots.

AFTER DETROIT eliminated Dallas, and Pittsburgh dispatched Philadelphia in the Conference Finals, we were left with two teams standing—a Stanley Cup Final showcasing the experienced, Presidents' Trophy–winning Red Wings and the youthful and explosive Penguins.

Detroit took a 2–0 series lead with back-to-back shutouts on home ice. Red Wings goalie Chris Osgood needed to make only 41 saves over the two games to frustrate the Pittsburgh offense. The experience of the Red Wings was clearly on display and working to their advantage.

The Penguins broke through in Game 3 for a 3–2 victory at Mellon Arena. Sidney Crosby led the attack with two goals, while Penguin goaltender Marc-Andre Fleury stood tall in the face of a mounting Detroit comeback by making 32 saves.

The pivotal Game 4 was a tense, cautious battle with each team realizing the magnitude of the outcome: a Detroit victory would mean they would need only one win in the final three games to clinch the Cup; a Pittsburgh victory would reduce the series to a best-of-three contest. Tied 1–1 only seven minutes into the first period, the score would remain that way until Jiri Hudler deposited a backhander past Fleury at 2:26 of the third period leading to a 2–1 victory.

Game 5 was a Cup game for the ages: beginning at 8:15 PM ET and ending with Petr Sykora's elimination-staving goal at 12:51 AM. Pittsburgh emerged as the victor in a 4–3 triple-overtime win, cancelling the celebration plans at Joe Louis Arena.

Adding to the lore of the fifth-longest game in Cup Final history was the story that emerged from the Pittsburgh locker room shortly after the crucial win. Apparently Sykora had said between periods that he would score the winning goal. Afterward he appeared almost embarrassed that his "called shot" story made it to the media.

"And about the shot, just between the periods, something stupid I said, just 'Guys, I'm just going to get one, so just don't worry about the game. I'm going to get a goal,'" Sykora admitted.

With two days to recover, the Red Wings put the bitter Game 5 disappointment behind them as they jumped out to a 2–0 lead and never trailed in a series-clinching 3–2 victory at Mellon Arena.

It was the 11th Stanley Cup title in franchise history and fourth since 1997.

Detroit's victory was historic in several ways. For starters, Swedish veteran Nicklas Lidstrom became the first European to captain a Stanley Cup winner. The defenseman had won the Cup three previous times, but watched Steve Yzerman accept the trophy. This time, Lidstrom was the one who got the party started.

"It felt great to be the first guy to touch the Cup on our team," he said. "I'm very proud of being the first European and of being the captain of the Red Wings."

Henrik Zetterberg, also a Swede, was awarded the Conn Smythe Trophy as MVP of the Stanley Cup Playoffs for scoring 13 goals and 27 points in 22 games. He became the second European-born and -trained player to win the honour, following in the footsteps of teammate Lidstrom, who won the Conn Smythe Trophy in 2002. Detroit's top-notch international scouting and farm system produced a record 12 Europeans—seven of them Swedes—who will have their names engraved on the Stanley Cup as 2008 champions.

Yes, it was quite a season. From the first faceoff to the lifting of the Stanley Cup, 2007–08 was filled with exciting, emotional, action-filled moments. Just turn the page for proof.

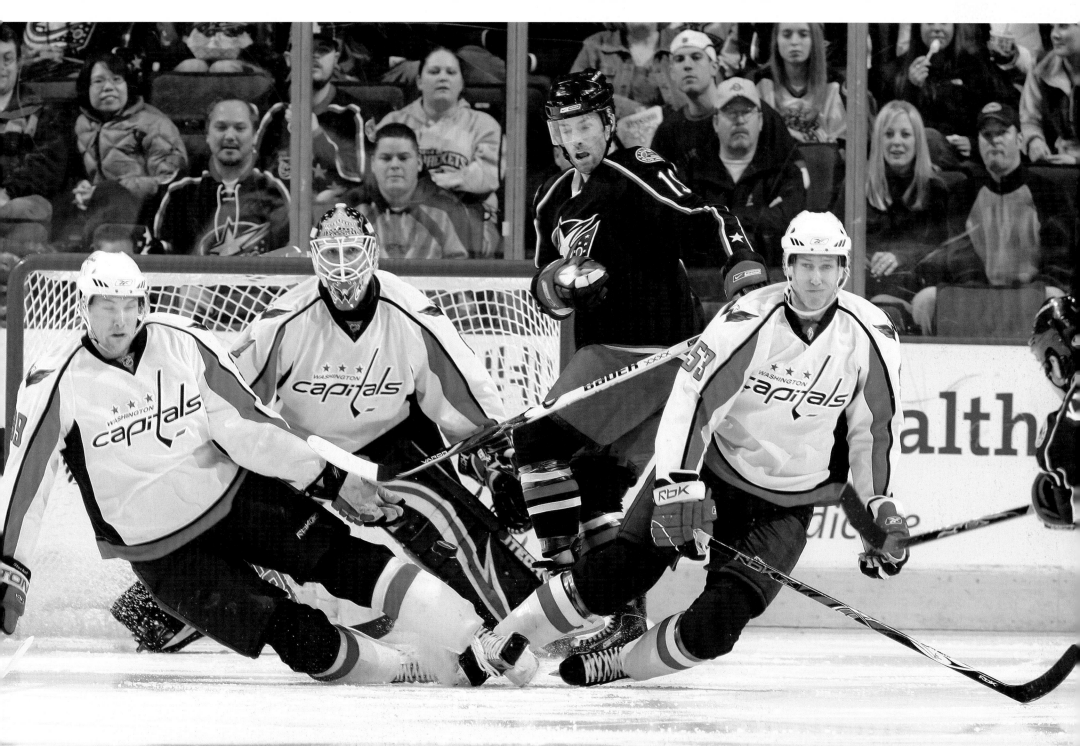

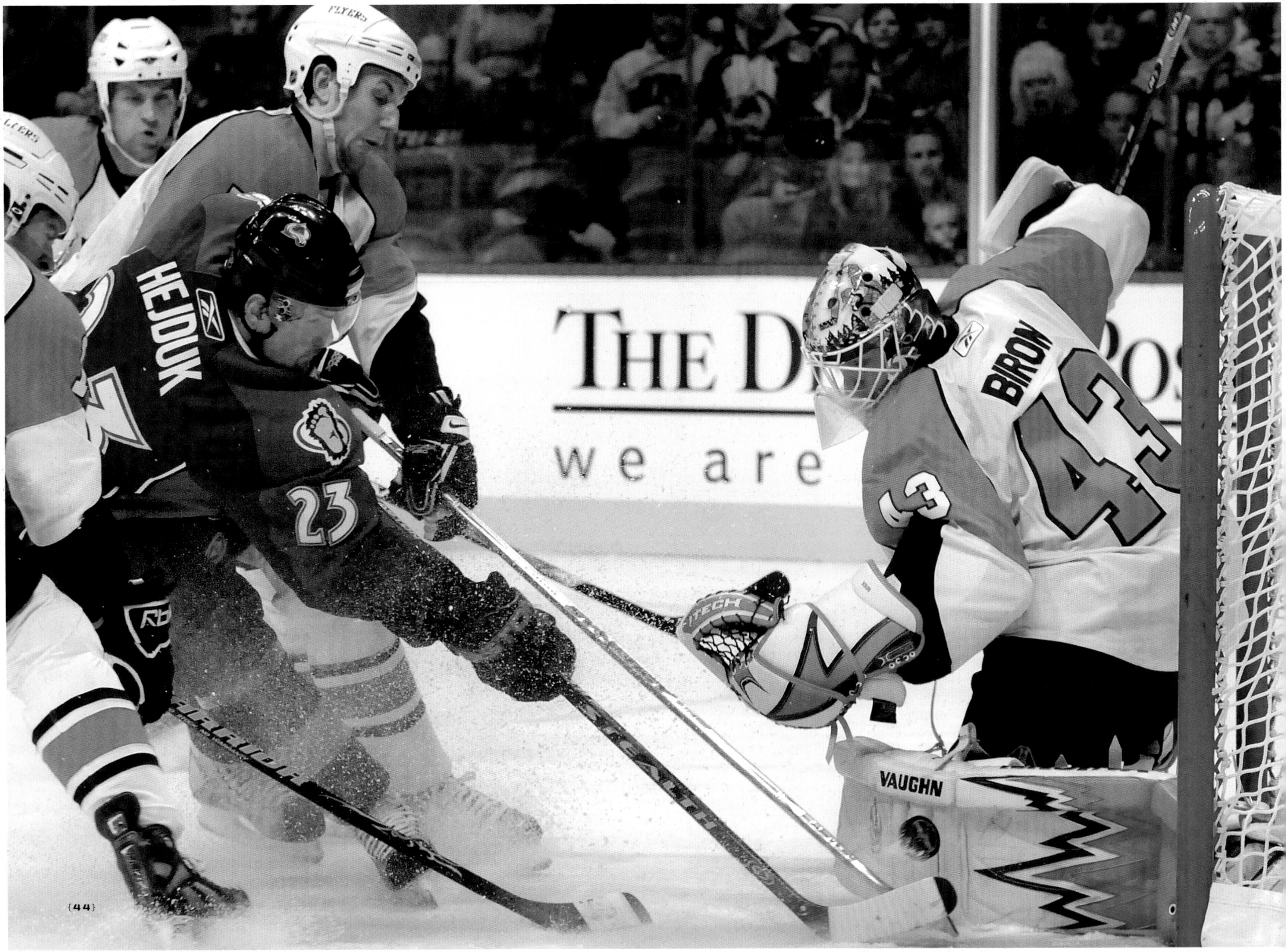
FLYERS
FLYERS
HEJDUK
23
THE D
we are
BIRON
43
VAUGHN

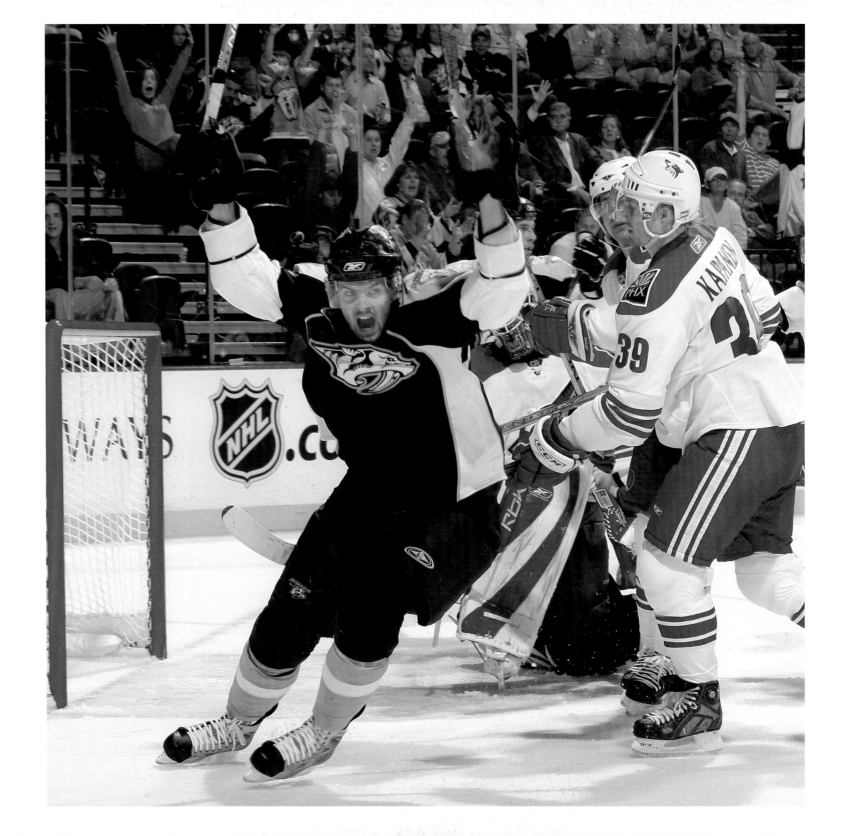

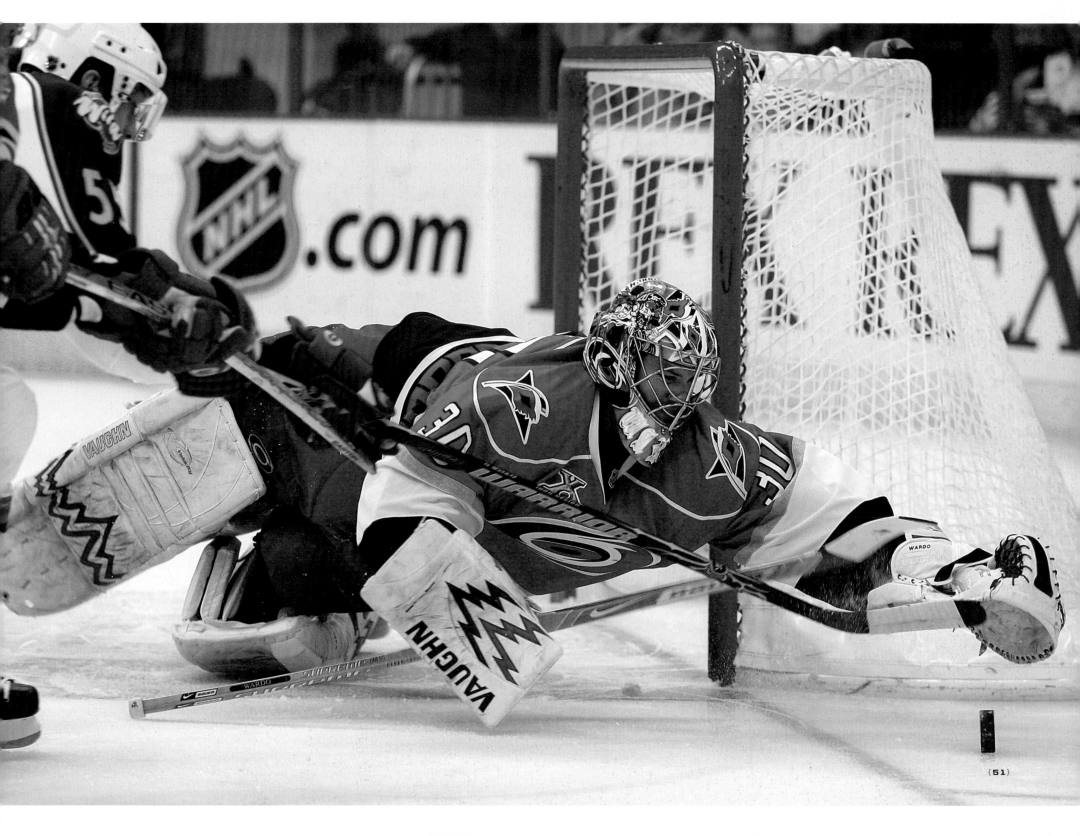

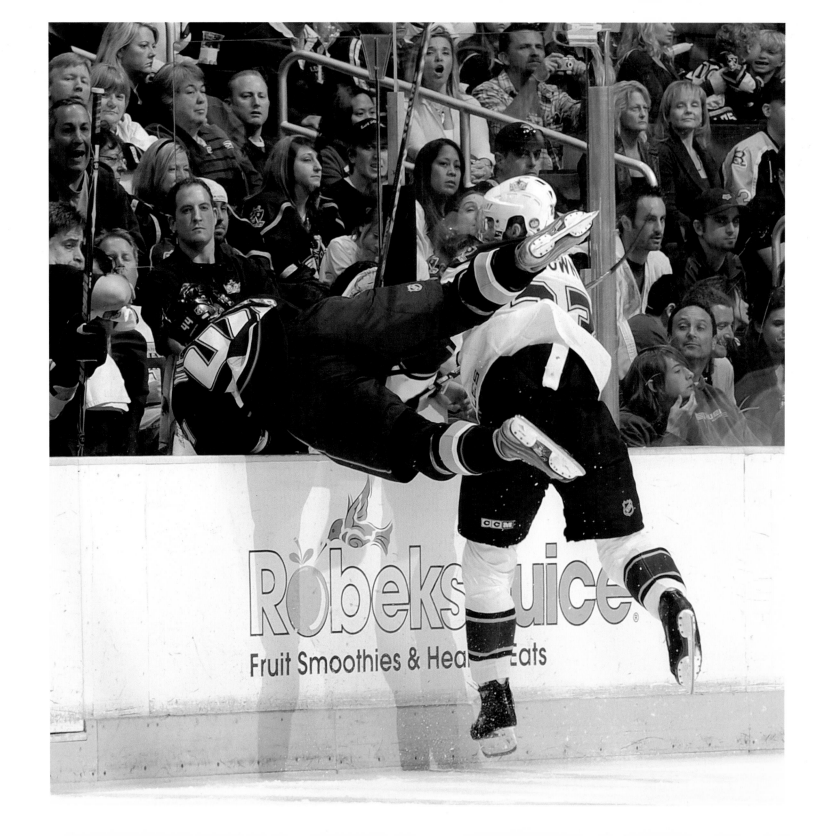

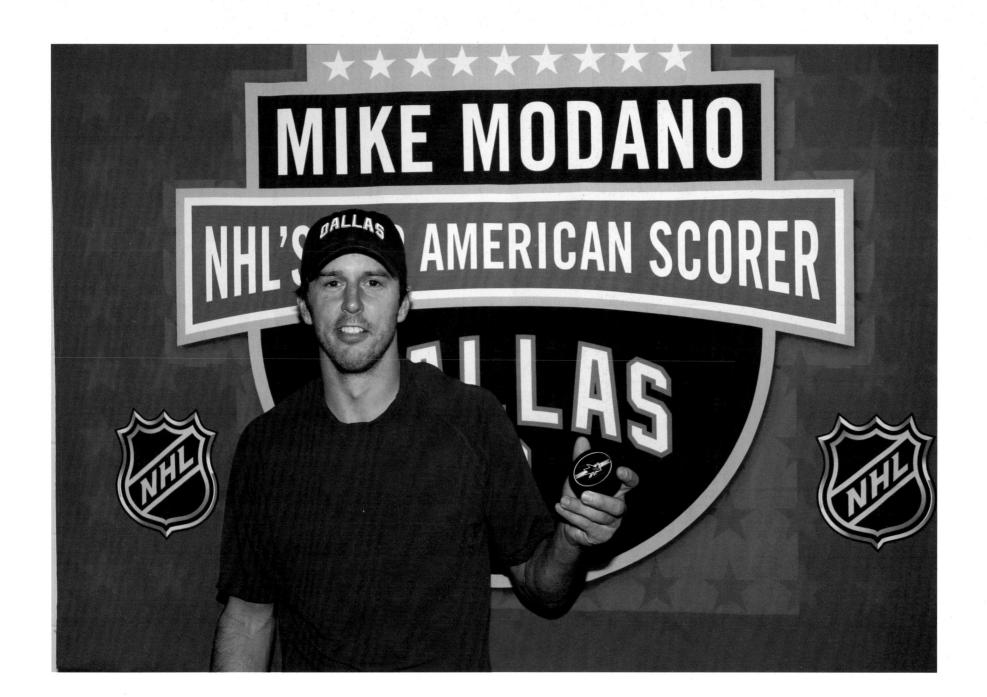

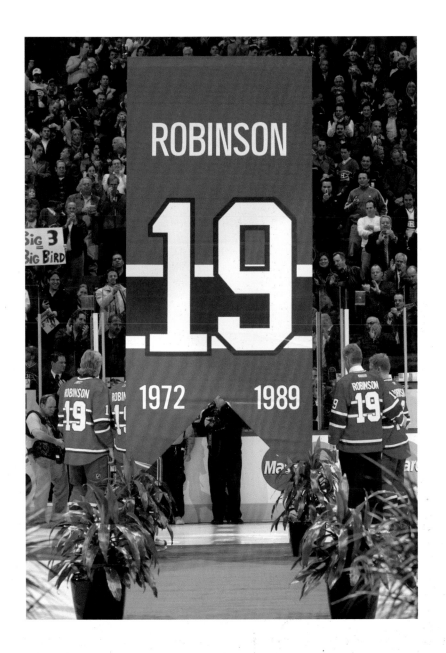

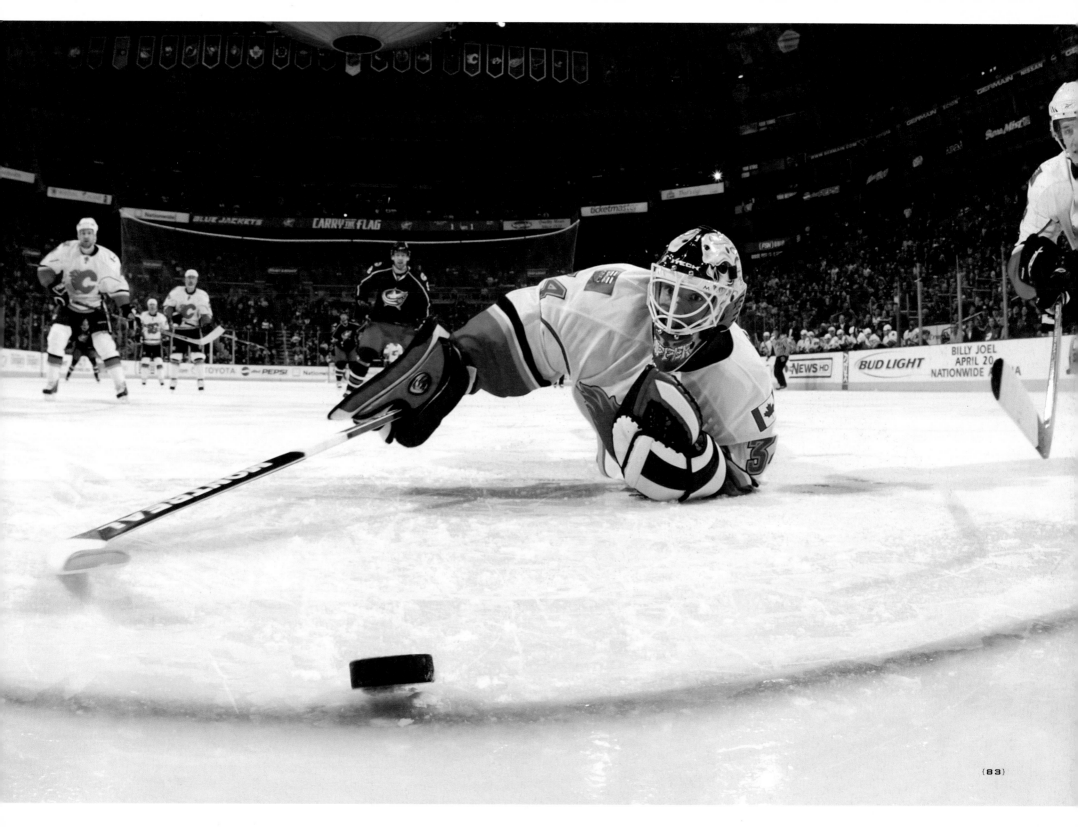

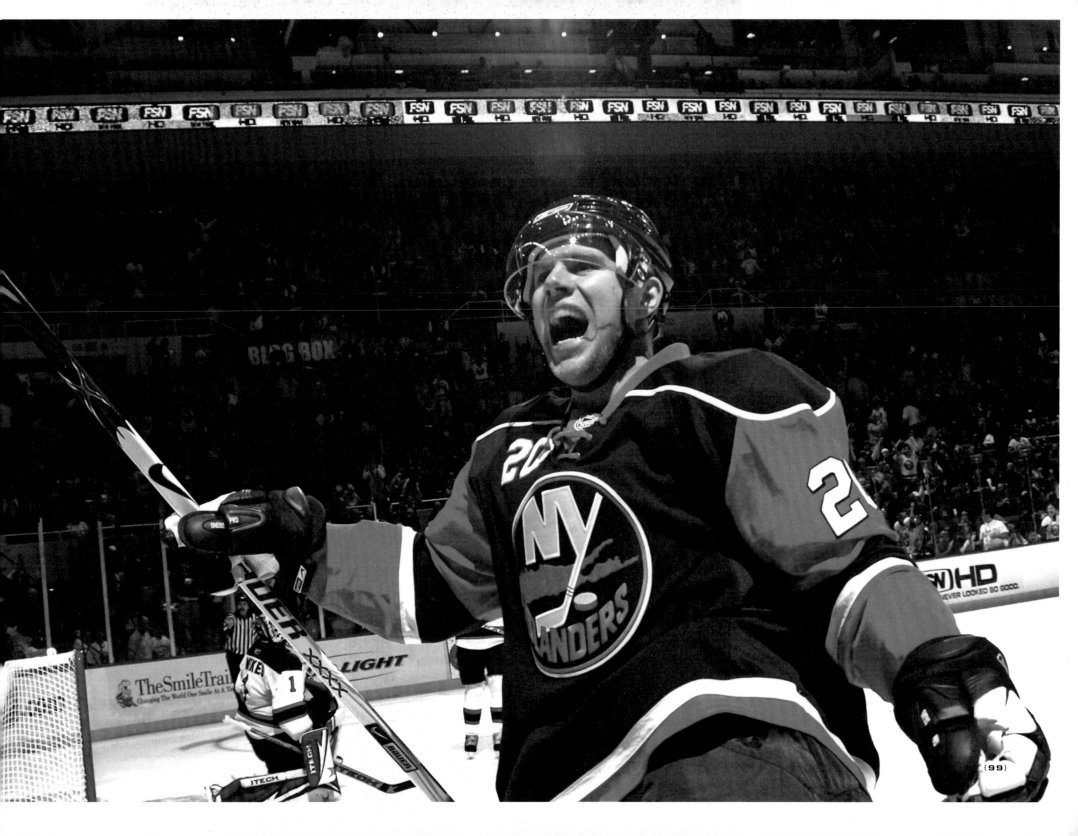

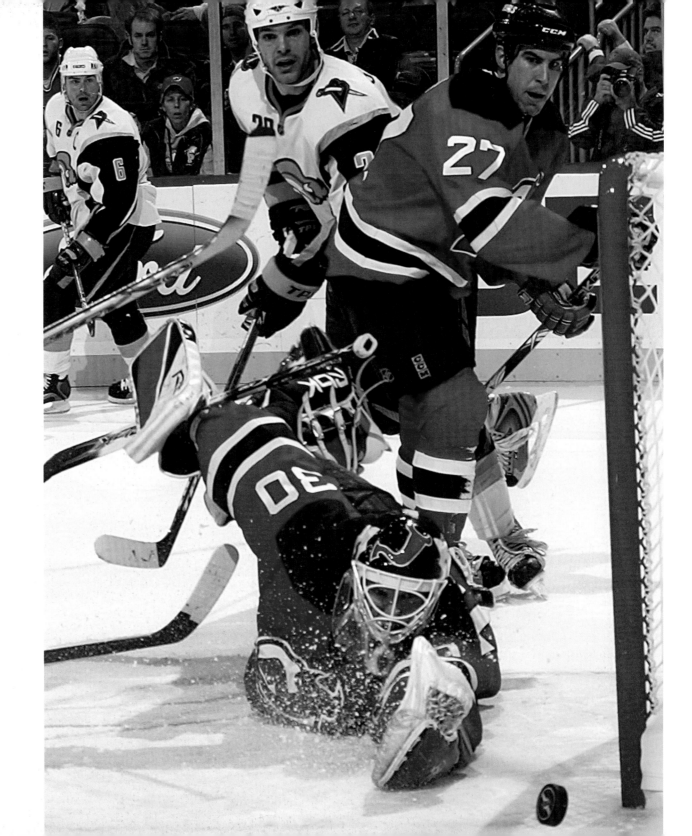

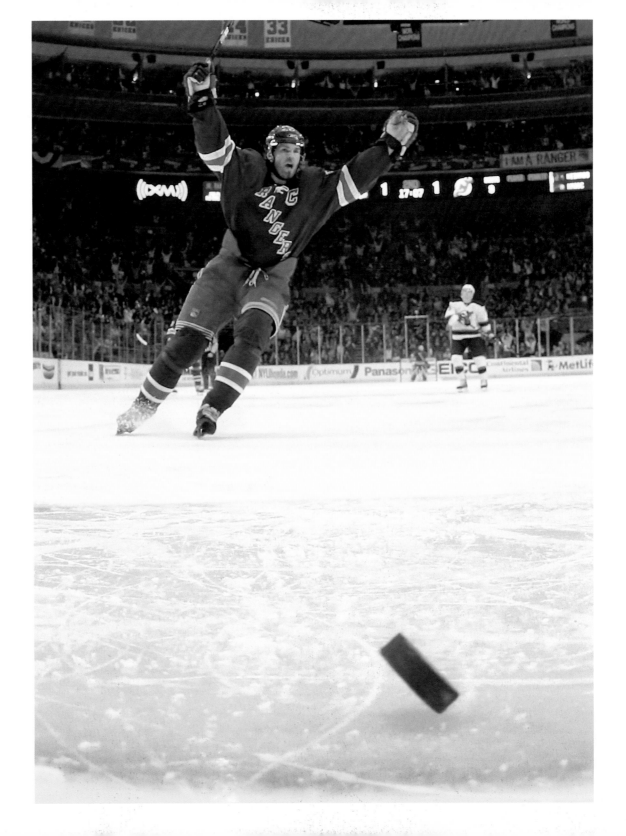

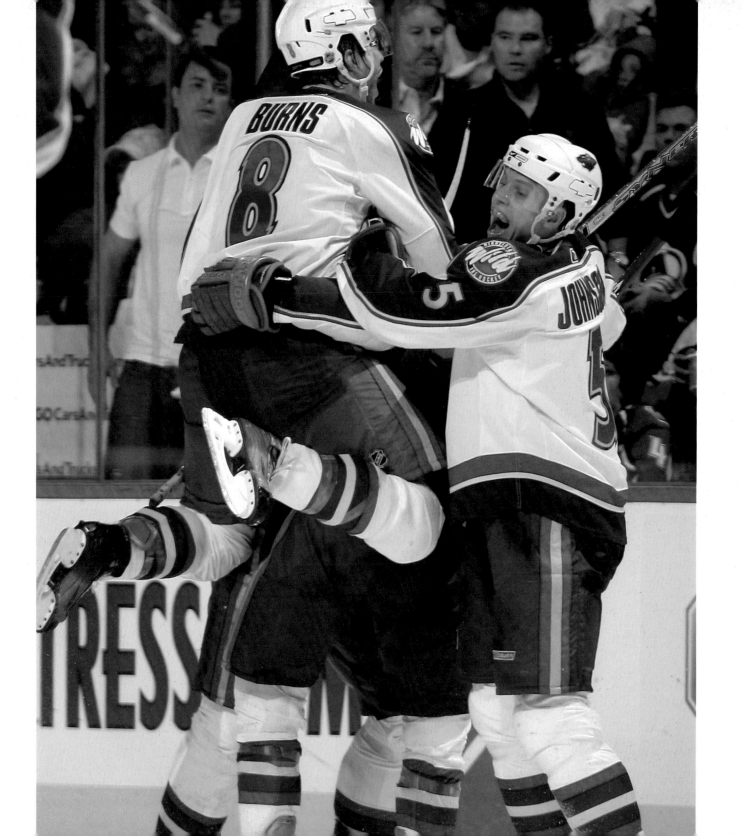

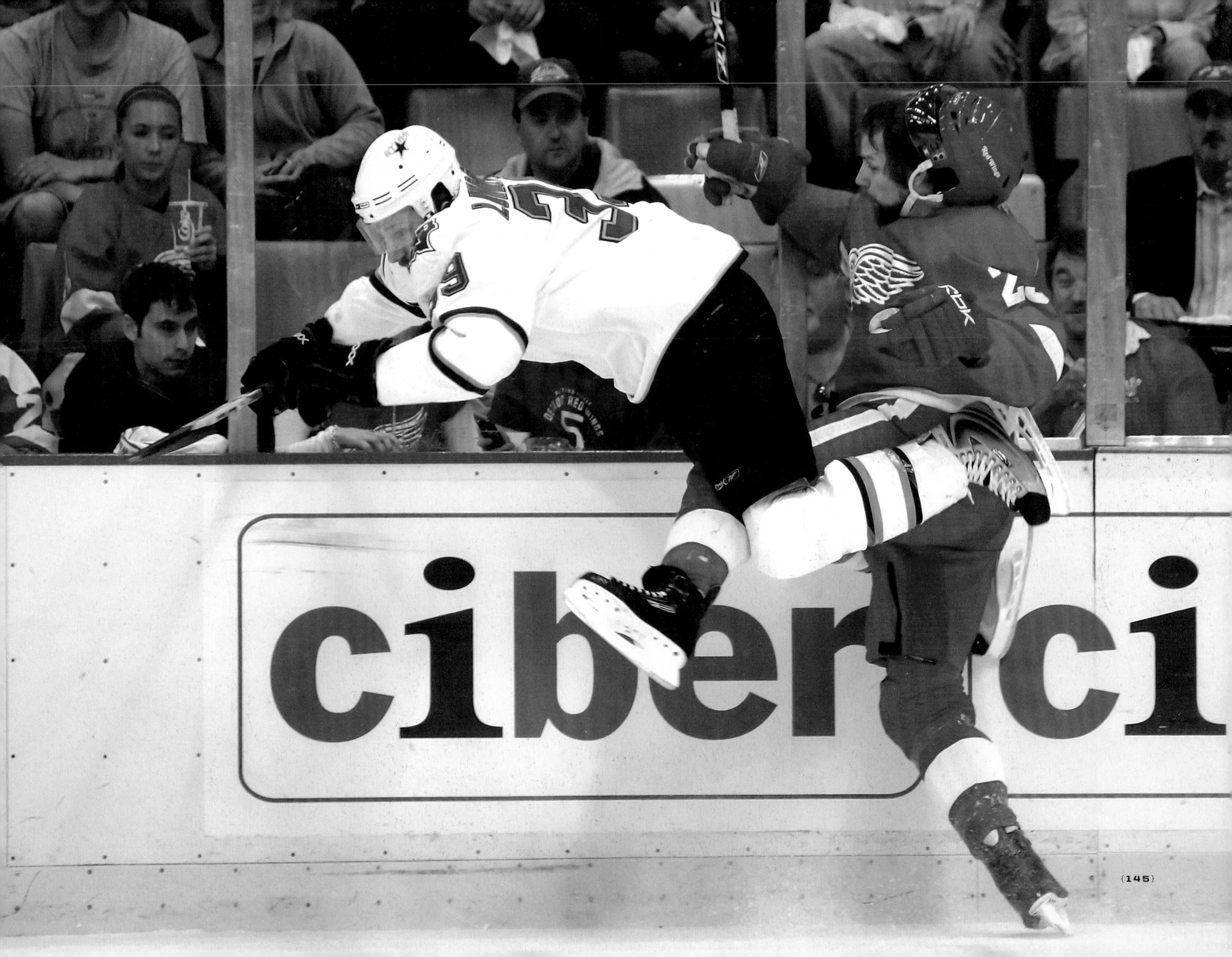

REGULAR SEASON STANDINGS

EASTERN CONFERENCE
ATLANTIC DIVISION

	W	L	OT	GF	GA	PTS
Pittsburgh (2)	47	27	8	247	216	102
New Jersey (4)	46	29	7	206	197	99
NY Rangers (5)	42	27	13	213	199	97
Philadelphia (6)	42	29	11	248	233	95
NY Islanders (13)	35	38	9	194	243	79

NORTHEAST DIVISION

	W	L	OT	GF	GA	PTS
Montreal (1)	47	25	10	262	222	104
Ottawa (7)	43	31	8	261	247	94
Boston (8)	41	29	12	212	222	94
Buffalo (10)	39	31	12	255	242	90
Toronto (12)	36	35	11	231	260	83

SOUTHEAST DIVISION

	W	L	OT	GF	GA	PTS
Washington (3)	43	31	8	242	231	94
Carolina (9)	43	33	6	252	249	92
Florida (11)	38	35	9	216	226	85
Atlanta (14)	34	40	8	216	272	76
Tampa Bay (15)	31	42	9	223	267	71

WESTERN CONFERENCE
CENTRAL DIVISION

	W	L	OT	GF	GA	PTS
Detroit (1)	54	21	7	257	184	115
Nashville (8)	41	32	9	230	229	91
Chicago (10)	40	34	8	239	235	88
Columbus (13)	34	36	12	193	218	80
St. Louis (14)	33	36	13	205	237	79

NORTHWEST DIVISION

	W	L	OT	GF	GA	PTS
Minnesota (3)	44	28	10	223	218	98
Colorado (6)	44	31	7	231	219	95
Calgary (7)	42	30	10	229	227	94
Edmonton (9)	41	35	6	235	251	88
Vancouver (11)	39	33	10	213	215	88

PACIFIC DIVISION

	W	L	OT	GF	GA	PTS
San Jose (2)	49	23	10	222	193	108
Anaheim (4)	47	27	8	205	191	102
Dallas (5)	45	30	7	242	207	97
Phoenix (12)	38	37	7	214	231	83
Los Angeles (15)	32	43	7	231	266	71

REGULAR SEASON
INDIVIDUAL STATS LEADERS

SCORING

Alexander Ovechkin (WSH)	112
Evgeni Malkin (PIT)	106
Jarome Iginla (CGY)	98
Pavel Datsyuk (DET)	97
Joe Thornton (SJS)	96
Henrik Zetterberg (DET)	92
Vincent Lecavalier (TBL)	92
Jason Spezza (OTT)	92
Daniel Alfredsson (OTT)	89
Ilya Kovalchuk (ATL)	87

SCORING (DEFENSEMEN)

Nicklas Lidstrom (DET)	70
Sergei Gonchar (PIT)	65
Mark Streit (MTL)	62
Brian Campbell (BUF-SJS)	62
Dion Phaneuf (CGY)	60
Andrei Markov (MTL)	58
Mike Green (WSH)	56
Brian Rafalski (DET)	55
Tomas Kaberle (TOR)	53
Zdeno Chara (BOS)	51
Ed Jovanovski (PHX)	51

GOALS

Alexander Ovechkin (WSH)	65
Ilya Kovalchuk (ATL)	52
Jarome Iginla (CGY)	50
Evgeni Malkin (PIT)	47

Henrik Zetterberg (DET)	43
Brad Boyes (STL)	43
Marian Gaborik (MIN)	42
Dany Heatley (OTT)	41
Vincent Lecavalier (TBL)	40
Daniel Alfredsson (OTT)	40

ASSISTS

Joe Thornton (SJS)	67
Pavel Datsyuk (DET)	66
Marc Savard (BOS)	63
Henrik Sedin (VAN)	61
Nicklas Lidstrom (DET)	60
Evgeni Malkin (PIT)	59
Jason Spezza (OTT)	58
Martin St. Louis (TBL)	58
Ryan Getzlaf (ANA)	58
Mike Ribeiro (DAL)	56

POWER-PLAY GOALS

Alexander Ovechkin (WSH)	22
Thomas Vanek (BUF)	19
Olli Jokinen (FLA)	18
Alex Kovalev (ATL)	17
Evgeni Malkin (PIT)	17
Henrik Zetterberg (DET)	16
Ilya Kovalchuk (ATL)	16
Jarome Iginla (CGY)	15
Mike Knuble (PHI)	15
Petr Sykora (PIT)	15

SHORTHANDED GOALS

Patrick Sharp (CHI)	7
Daniel Alfredsson (OTT)	7
Rene Bourque (CHI)	5
Mike Richards (PHI)	5
Richard Park (NYI)	4
Niklas Hagman (DAL)	4
Rick Nash (CBJ)	4

GAME-WINNING GOALS

Alexander Ovechkin (WSH)	11
Jeremy Roenick (SJS)	10
Thomas Vanek (BUF)	9
Jarome Iginla (CGY)	9
Brad Boyes (STL)	9

PLUS/MINUS

Pavel Datsyuk (DET)	+41
Nicklas Lidstrom (DET)	+40
Dany Heatley (OTT)	+33
Ryan Getzlaf (ANA)	+32
Henrik Zetterberg (DET)	+30
Duncan Keith (CHI)	+30
Alexander Ovechkin (WSH)	+28
Viktor Kozlov (WSH)	+28
Brian Rafalski (DET)	+27
Jarome Iginla (CGY)	+27
Johnny Oduya (NJD)	+27

GOALTENDING LEADERS

WINS

Evgeni Nabokov (SJS)	46
Martin Brodeur (NJD)	44
Miikka Kiprusoff (CGY)	39
Henrik Lundqvist (NYR)	37
Cam Ward (CAR)	37

GOALS-AGAINST AVERAGE

Chris Osgood (DET)	2.09
J.S. Giguere (ANA)	2.12
Evgeni Nabokov (SJS)	2.14
Dominik Hasek (DET)	2.14
Martin Brodeur (NJD)	2.17

SAVE PERCENTAGE

Dan Ellis (NSH)	.924
Ty Conklin (PIT)	.923
J.S. Giguere (ANA)	.922
Tim Thomas (BOS)	.921
Marc-Andre Fleury (PIT)	.921

SHUTOUTS

Henrik Lundqvist (NYR)	10
Pascal Leclaire (CBJ)	9
Evgeni Nabokov (SJS)	6
Roberto Luongo (VAN)	6
Dan Ellis (NSH)	6

STANLEY CUP PLAYOFFS

EASTERN CONFERENCE   **WESTERN CONFERENCE**

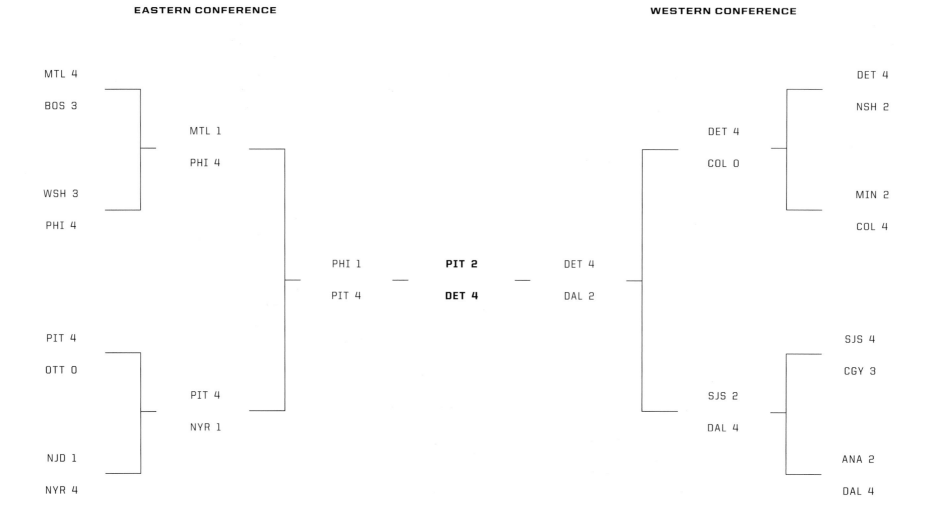

MTL 4

BOS 3

MTL 1

PHI 4

WSH 3

PHI 4

PHI 1

PIT 4

PIT 2

DET 4

DET 4

DAL 2

PIT 4

OTT 0

PIT 4

NYR 1

NJD 1

NYR 4

DET 4

COL 0

SJS 2

DAL 4

DET 4

NSH 2

MIN 2

COL 4

SJS 4

CGY 3

ANA 2

DAL 4

HONOURS AND AWARDS

NHL FIRST ALL-STAR TEAM
G—Evgeni Nabokov (SJS)
D—Nicklas Lidstrom (DET)
D—Dion Phaneuf (CGY)
C—Evgeni Malkin (PIT)
RW—Jarome Iginla (CGY)
LW—Alexander Ovechkin (WSH)

NHL SECOND ALL-STAR TEAM
G—Martin Brodeur (NJD)
D—Brian Campbell (BUF-SJS)
D—Zdeno Chara (BOS)
C—Joe Thornton (SJS)
RW—Alex Kovalev (MTL)
LW—Henrik Zetterberg (DET)

PRESIDENTS' TROPHY
Best Overall Record:
Detroit Red Wings

PRINCE OF WALES TROPHY
Eastern Conference Champion:
Pittsburgh Penguins

CLARENCE S. CAMPBELL BOWL
Western Conference Champion:
Detroit Red Wings

ART ROSS TROPHY
Top Point Scorer in the NHL:
Alexander Ovechkin (WSH)

BILL MASTERTON MEMORIAL TROPHY
Qualities of Perseverance
and Sportsmanship:
Jason Blake (TOR)

CALDER MEMORIAL TROPHY
Rookie of the Year:
Patrick Kane (CHI)

CONN SMYTHE TROPHY
Most Valuable Player
in the Stanley Cup Playoffs:
Henrik Zetterberg (DET)

FRANK J. SELKE TROPHY
Top Defensive Forward:
Pavel Datsyuk (DET)

HART MEMORIAL TROPHY
NHL Most Valuable Player:
Alexander Ovechkin (WSH)

JACK ADAMS AWARD
Coach of the Year:
Bruce Boudreau (WSH)

JAMES NORRIS MEMORIAL TROPHY
Top Defenseman:
Nicklas Lidstrom (DET)

KING CLANCY MEMORIAL TROPHY
Leadership and Humanitarian
Contribution: Vincent Lecavalier (TBL)

LADY BYNG MEMORIAL TROPHY
Player Who Displays Gentlemanly
Conduct: Pavel Datsyuk (DET)

LESTER B. PEARSON AWARD
Most Outstanding Player as
Selected by the NHLPA:
Alexander Ovechkin (WSH)

LESTER PATRICK TROPHY
Outstanding Service to Hockey
in the United States:
Brian Leetch
Cammi Granato
Stan Fischler
John Halligan

MAURICE RICHARD TROPHY
Top Goal Scorer:
Alexander Ovechkin (WSH)

VEZINA TROPHY
Top Goaltender:
Martin Brodeur (NJD)

WILLIAM M. JENNINGS TROPHY
Goaltender(s) with the Fewest Goals
Scored Against: Dominik Hasek/
Chris Osgood (DET)

2008 NHL ENTRY DRAFT

FIRST ROUND

CLUB	PLAYER	BIRTHPLACE	AMATEUR LEAGUE	AMATEUR CLUB	POS
1 TBL	Steven Stamkos	Markham, ON	OHL	Sarnia	C
2 LAK	Drew Doughty	London, ON	OHL	Guelph	D
3 ATL	Zach Bogosian	Massena, NY	OHL	Peterborough	D
4 STL	Alex Pietrangelo	King City, ON	OHL	Niagara	D
5 TOR	Luke Schenn	Saskatoon, SK	WHL	Kelowna	D
6 CBJ	Nikita Filatov	Moscow, Russia	RUSSIA-3	CSKA 2	LW
7 NSH	Colin Wilson	Greenwich, CT	H-EAST	Boston University	C
8 PHX	Mikkel Boedker	Brondby, Denmark	OHL	Kitchener	LW
9 NYI	Joshua Bailey	Oshawa, ON	OHL	Windsor	C
10 VAN	Cody Hodgson	Toronto, ON	OHL	Brampton	C
11 CHI	Kyle Beach	Vancouver, BC	WHL	Everett	C
12 BUF	Tyler Myers	Houston, TX	WHL	Kelowna	D
13 LAK	Colten Teubert	White Rock, BC	WHL	Regina	D
14 CAR	Zach Boychuk	Calgary, AB	WHL	Lethbridge	C
15 OTT	Erik Karlsson	Landsbro, Sweden	SWE-JR.	Frolunda Jr.	D
16 BOS	Joe Colborne	Calgary, AB	AJHL	Camrose	C
17 ANA	Jake Gardiner	Deephaven, MN	HIGH-MN	Minnetonka	D
18 NSH	Chet Pickard	Moncton, NB	WHL	Tri-City	G
19 PHI	Luca Sbisa	Oberageri, Switzerland	WHL	Lethbridge	D
20 NYR	Michael Del Zotto	Stouffville, ON	OHL	Oshawa	D
21 WSH	Anton Gustafsson	Karlskoga, Sweden	SWE-JR.	Frolunda Jr.	C
22 EDM	Jordan Eberle	Regina, SK	WHL	Regina	C
23 MIN	Tyler Cuma	Toronto, ON	OHL	Ottawa	D
24 NJD	Mattias Tedenby	Vetlanda, Sweden	SWEDEN	HV 71	LW
25 CGY	Greg Nemisz	Courtice, ON	OHL	Windsor	C
26 BUF	Tyler Ennis	Edmonton, AB	WHL	Medicine Hat	C
27 WSH	John Carlson	Natick, MA	USHL	Indiana	D
28 PHX	Viktor Tikhonov	Moscow, Russia	RUSSIA	Cherepovets	W
29 ATL	Daultan Leveille	St. Catharines, ON	GHL	St. Catharines	C
30 DET	Thomas Mccollum	Amherst, NY	OHL	Guelph	G

IMAGE CAPTIONS AND CREDITS

All photographs by NHL images and Getty Images.

2   *Two Islanders cast long shadows during pre-game introductions.* January 15, 2008 Nassau Coliseum in Uniondale, NY Photo: Jim McIsaac

5   *Alexander Ovechkin.* October 8, 2007 Nassau Coliseum in Uniondale, NY Photo: Bruce Bennett

8   *Islander Chris Campoli puts on the breaks.* January 19, 2008, General Motors Place in Vancouver, BC; Photo: Jeff Vinnick

16   *Sabres players collect their thoughts before a game.* October 15, 2007, HSBC Arena in Buffalo, NY; Photo: Bill Wippert

17   *Kirk Maltby and Dallas Drake discuss strategy with Chris Osgood during intermission.* November 9, 2007, Joe Louis Arena in Detroit, MI; Photo: Dave Reginek

18   *Toronto's Hall Gill gets warm-ups underway.* September 24, 2007, Air Canada Centre in Toronto, ON; Photo: Dave Sandford

19   *Ottawa's Luke Richardson stretches solo in the Senators' hallway.* February 25, 2008 Scotiabank Place in Ottawa, ON Photo: Andre Ringuette

20   *Detroit's Kris Draper sends pucks flying onto the ice to start pre-game warm-ups.* March 11, 2008, Joe Louis Arena in Detroit, MI Photo: Dave Reginek

21   *Corey Perry of the Ducks dishes out a few pucks.* February 5, 2008, Nassau Coliseum in Uniondale, NY; Photo: Bruce Bennett

22   *L.A.'s Jack Johnson runs the gauntlet of King's fans.* November 3, 2007 Staples Center in Los Angeles, CA Photo: Noah Graham

23   *Canucks goalie Roberto Luongo glows under the lights.* February 14, 2008 General Motors Place in Vancouver, BC Photo: Jeff Vinnick

24   *Columbus Blue Jackets goalie Pascal Leclaire is all focus.* January 20, 2008, Pepsi Center in Denver, CO Photo: Doug Pensinger

25   *The spotlight shines on San Jose Sharks goalie Evgeni Nabakov.* November 7, 2007 HP Pavilion in San Jose, CA Photo: Jed Jacobsohn

26   *Shark attack: San Jose's Craig Rivet emerges.* December 20, 2007 HP Pavilion in San Jose, CA Photo: Christian Petersen

27   *Two young Sabres fans cheer for their beloved team.* February 8, 2008 HSBC Arena in Buffalo, NY Photo: Bill Wippert

28   *Keith Tkachuk of the St. Louis Blues is introduced to the crowd.* October 10, 2007 Scottrade Center in St. Louis, MO Photo: Mark Buckner

29   *Anaheim's J.S. Giguere takes the first step on freshly surfaced ice.* November 25, 2007, Honda Center in Anaheim, CA Photo: Christian Petersen

30   *Oilers' captain Ethan Moreau eyes down his opponent in the faceoff circle.* January 13, 2008, Rexall Place in Edmonton, AB Photo: Andy Devlin

31   *Mattias Norstrom of the Dallas Stars prepares for the faceoff.* October 25, 2007 Staples Center in Los Angeles, CA Photo: Victor Decolongon

32   *London bridges: The NHL kicked off the 2007–08 regular season overseas in London.* September 29, 2007 O2 Arena in London, England Photo: Daniel Berehulak

33   *Rostislav Olesz hears it from the crowd.* February 21, 2008, BankAtlantic Center in Sunrise, FL; Photo: Al Messerschmidt

34   *Bryce Salvador looks to provide solid defensive zone coverage.* March 11, 2008 Bell Centre in Montreal, QC Photo: Dave Sandford

35   *Phoenix goalie Ilya Bryzgalov of Phoenix is congratulated by teammate Peter Mueller.* January 11, 2008 , General Motors Place in Vancouver, BC; Photo: Jeff Vinnick

36   *Maxim Talbot of the Penguins soars through the crease of Buffalo goalie Ryan Miller* February 17, 2008, HSBC Arena in Buffalo, NY; Photo: Bill Wippert

37   *Columbus goalie Pascal Leclaire cannot avoid Vancouver's Mason Raymond.* February 29, 2008, General Motors Place in Vancouver, BC Photo: Jeff Vinnick

38   *Steve Begin is full speed ahead on the Canadiens forecheck.* November 23, 2007 HSBC Arena in Buffalo, NY Photo: Dave Sandford

39   Capitals blueliners make way for goalie Brent Johnson. February 5, 2008 Nationwide Arena in Columbus, OH Photo: Jamie Sabau

40   *Saku Koivu raises his arms in front of a fallen teammate to celebrate another Montreal goal.* February 19, 2008 Bell Centre in Montreal, QC Photo:

41   *Red Wings captain Nicklas Lidstrom lunges to keep the puck from two Coyotes in pursuit.* January 30, 2008, Joe Louis Arena in Detroit, MI; Photo: Dave Reginek

42   *Oilers enforcer Zach Stortini goes around the corner to get one past J.S. Giguere.* December 2, 2007, Honda Center in Anaheim, CA; Photo: Jeff Gross

43   *Tyler Arnason goes airborne as he releases a wrist shot versus Edmonton.* November 7, 2007, General Motors Place in Vancouver, BC; Photo: Michael Martin

44   *Milan Hejduk gets the shot off in close quarters.* December 7, 2007, Pepsi Center in Denver, CO; Photo: Steve Dykes

45   *Carolina star Eric Staal tries to stuff the puck past Panthers' goalie Tomas Vokoun.* April 7, 2008, RBC Center in Raleigh, NC; Photo: Gregg Forwerck

46   *Flyers forward Daniel Briere collides with New Jersey's Mike Mottau.* September 24, 2007, Wachovia Center in Philadelphia, PA; Photo: Len Redkoles

47   *Snow storm: Rick Nash of Columbus and Wild defenseman Nick Shultz battle for the puck along the boards.* October 6, 2007 Xcel Energy Center in St. Paul, MN Photo: Scott A. Schneider

48   *Predators forward Alexander Radulov celebrates a huge goal in front of the home crowd.* October 11, 2007, Sommet Center in Nashville, TN; Photo: John Russell

49   *Marc Savard gives a big fist pump as he celebrates a Bruins goal.* November 1, 2007 TD Banknorth Garden in Boston, MA Photo: Elsa

50   *Travis Zajac of the Devils looks on as Islanders' goalie Rick DiPietro sprawls to keep the puck out of the net.* January 16, 2008, Prudential Center in Newark, NJ Photo: Bruce Bennett

51   *Hurricanes goaltender Cam Ward pounces on a loose puck.* March 6, 2008, RBC Center in Raleigh, NC; Photo: Kevin C. Cox

52   *Flames captain Jarome Iginla pins Jonathan Cheechoo along the boards.* September 25, 2007, Pengrowth Saddledome in Calgary, AB; Photo: Tim Smith

93 *Hurricanes' Chad LaRose never takes his eye off the puck.* January 5, 2008, Scottrade Center in St. Louis, MO
Photo: Mark Buckner

94 *Daniel Briere of the Flyers sets up for the faceoff.* September 24, 2007
Wachovia Center in Philadelphia, PA
Photo: Len Redkoles

95 *Tampa Bay's Paul Ranger can't get past the Leafs' Jason Blake.* December 10, 2007
Air Canada Centre in Toronto, ON
Photo: Graig Abel

96 *Pittsburgh's Sidney Crosby stickhandles through the New Jersey defense.*
October 17, 2007, Mellon Arena in Pittsburgh, PA; Photo: Gregory Shamus

97 *St. Louis's Manny Legace celebrates after shutting out Anaheim.* February 1, 2008
Scottrade Center in St. Louis, MO
Photo: Mark Buckner

98 *Sidney Crosby after another goal.*
October 13, 2007, Air Canada Centre in Toronto, ON; Photo: Graig Abel

99 *Islanders' Sean Bergenheim salutes the home crowd after a goal.* October 20, 2007
Nassau Coliseum in Uniondale, NY
Photo: Bruce Bennett

100 *Jordan Staal of the Penguins uses his quick release to get off a shot.* February 26, 2008
Nassau Coliseum in Uniondale, NY
Photo: Jim McIsaac

101 *Tampa Bay's Michel Ouellet jams the puck past Cristobal Huet of the Canadiens.*
February 12, 2008, St. Pete Times in Tampa, FL; Photo: Bruce Bennett

102 *Mike Comrie of the Islanders puts a backhand past the Leafs' Andrew Raycraft.*
December 26, 2007, Nassau Coliseum in Uniondale, NY; Photo: Bruce Bennett

103 *Florida's Craig Anderson sprawls to keep the puck out of his net.* January 3, 2008
Nassau Coliseum in Uniondale, NY
Photo: Melanie Bennett

104 *Jeremy Reich of the Bruins skates against the Devils.* December 5, 2007,
Prudential Center in Newark, NJ
Photo: Jim McIsaac

105 *Ilya Kovulchuk of Atlanta hops past Pittsburgh's Ryan Malone.* January 12, 2008
Philips Arena in Atlanta, GA
Photo: Scott Cunningham

106 *Montreal's Tomas Plekanec celebrates a goal against Nashville.* December 1, 2007
Bell Centre in Montreal, QC
Photo: Andre Ringuette

107 *Ottawa Senators rejoice after a goal against the Sabres.* December 26, 2007
HSBC Arena in Buffalo, NY
Photo: Bill Wippert

108 *A scoring opportunity for the Sabres goes just wide.* January 8, 2008
Prudential Center in Newark, NJ
Photo: Bruce Bennett

109 *Sharks' Jonathan Cheechoo crashes into Stars' goalie Marty Turco.* May 2, 2008
HP Pavilion in San Jose, CA
Photo: Don Smith

110 *Kings' Mike Cammalleri flips the puck over the shoulder of Oiler goalie Mathieu Garon.*
December 3, 2007, Staples Center in Los Angeles, CA; Photo: Jeff Gross

111 *Steve Downie of the Flyers celebrates a goal against the Rangers.* January 10, 2008
Madison Square Garden in New York, NY
Photo: Bruce Bennett

112 *The Ottawa Senators bench celebrates after a goal.* November 6, 2007
Scotiabank Place in Ottawa, ON
Photo: Andre Ringuette

113 *Tomas Holmstrom returns to the Detroit bench after a Red Wings goal.* December 9, 2007, Joe Louis Arena in Detroit, MI
Photo: Dave Reginek

114 *Alexander Ovechkin shows his youthful exuberance after a goal in his first Stanley Cup Playoff appearance.* April 25, 2008
Wachovia Center in Philadelphia, PA
Photo: Len Redkoles

115 *The city of Detroit showing their Red Wings pride.* April 18, 2008, Joe Louis Arena in Detroit, MI; Photo: Gregory Shamus

116 *Dennis Wideman catches Marc Savard after a Bruins tally.* April 13, 2008
TD Banknorth Garden in Boston, MA
Photo: Elsa

117 *Nicklas Lidstom and Chris Chelios have their game faces on.* April 10, 2008
Joe Louis Arena in Detroit, MI
Photo: Dave Reginek

118 *John-Michael Liles tees it up with traffic in front.* April 11, 2008, Xcel Energy Center in St. Paul, MN; Photo: Bruce Kluckhohn

119 *Robyn Regehr of the Flames and Patrick Rissmiller of the Sharks fight for the puck.*
April 9, 2008 , HP Pavilion at San Jose in San Jose, CA ; Photo: Don Smith

120 *Dany Heatley lunges to knock the puck away from Pittsburgh's Evgeni Malkin.* April 9, 2008, Mellon Arena in Pittsburgh, PA
Photo: Gregory Shamus

121 *New Jersey head coach Brent Sutter lets the officials know his disapproval of the call.*
April 11, 2008, Prudential Center in Newark, NJ; Photo: Jim McIsaac

122 *Joffrey Lupul is ecstatic after putting home a rebound to clinch Game 7 against the Capitals.* April 22, 2008, Verizon Center in Washington, DC; Photo: Len Redkoles

123 *Paul Martin of New Jersey and Sean Avery of the Rangers go flying over Devil's goaltender Martin Brodeur.* April 18, 2008
Prudential Center in Newark, NJ
Photo: Andy Marlin

124 *Canadiens goaltender Carey Price throws his glove hand out in an attempt to make an acrobatic save.* April 19, 2008
TD Banknorth Garden in Boston, MA
Photo: Elsa

125 *Montreal Canadiens leap for joy as they celebrate a goal.* April 19, 2008
TD Banknorth Garden in Boston, MA
Photo: Elsa

126 *Joe Pavelski of the Sharks celebrates a San Jose playoff goal.* April 17, 2008
HP Pavilion in San Jose, CA
Photo: Don Smith

127 *Daniel Alfredsson shakes the hand of Pittsburgh defenseman Brooks Orpik moments after the first round.* April 16, 2008
Scotiabank Place in Ottawa, ON
Photo: Andre Ringuette

128 *Jaromir Jagr raises his arms after a victory against cross-town rival New Jersey Devils.*
April 16, 2008, Madison Square Garden in New York, NY; Photo: Bruce Bennett

129 *San Jose all-star Joe Thornton is greeted with open arms by his teammates following a Sharks goal.* April 15, 2008
Pengrowth Saddledome in Calgary, AB
Photo: Mike Ridewood

130 *Vitaly Vishnevski and Frederik Sjostrom are in a deep battle in front of Martin Brodeur.*
April 16, 2008, Madison Square Garden in New York, NY; Photo:

131 *Members of the Minnesota Wild celebrate an overtime goal.* April 14, 2008
Pepsi Center in Denver, CO
Photo: Doug Pensinger

132 *Al the Octopus looks over the Red Wing's first round match up with the Nashville Predators.* May 17, 2008
Joe Louis Arena in Detroit, MI
Photo: Gregory Shamus

133 *Dan Cleary of the Red Wings looks for a rebound off Dan Ellis of the Predators.*
April 20, 2008 , Sommet Center in Nashville, TN ; Photo: Bruce Bennett

134 *Joe Pavelski and Patrick Marleau of the San Jose Sharks come together after a goal.*
May 2, 2008, HP Pavilion in San Jose, CA; Photo: Don Smith

135 *Pittsburgh's Ryan Whitney bear hugs newcomer Marian Hossa after advancing to the Stanley Cup Finals.* May 4, 2008
Mellon Arena in Pittsburgh, PA
Photo: Gregory Shamus